BACKLASH
PRESS

A pioneering publishing house dedicated to creating intelligent, vivid books.

Established to inform, educate,

entertain and provoke.

Journal Four

A Backlash Book
First published 2020

Backlash Press
71 Goldstone Crescent, Hove, England, BN3 6LS

ISBN: 978-1-9162666-9-8

www.backlashpress.com
info@backlashpress.com

Designer:
The Scrutineer, Rachael Adams.
Fonts: Baskerville, Bree serif.
Printed and bound by IngramSpark

All rights reserved. No part of this publication may be reproduced, stored in a retrieval system or transmitted in any form or by any means, electronic, mechanical, photocopying, recording or otherwise, without permission of the copyright holder.

Copyright © Gretchen Heffernan 2020
The moral rights of the contributors have been asserted.

Contents

Christopher Hopkins	5
Nick Cirkovic	9
Claire Scott	20
Annie McCrea	28
Bruce Bromley	33
Dorian Nightingale	40
Gret Heffernan	44

Christopher Hopkins

Gentle Winter Fox

Pellet bone and skin
like a love song under the coral oak
in the night of pale but of absent moon.
Spring alight in the eyes and strut
this poppy grin of walking fire
this purposed dog of a winter's hunt.

The cold has devoured the sound
trapped it under the sea glass ponds,
less the bark of the happy mutt
and a gentle hush from the cinder line
the salt brown track where the beauty spoils.
The sun has been lock out
now the world is an iceberg
our world is a bowl.

His quicken step, nose down
up the slippery common marble
of pavements from spindrift heels
with the stars above
but not of heaven high
these council sparkles of lamppost hung

the vailed contours of the curb side long.
the dusted rubbish
of the salt dregs of town
there sit bare fingers
under the duvet mounds.

the nested home of the moved along.

The mute spring colours are their
rags of living though we talk of
them like the dead.

And as the wishbones split
with a marrow crack
like the snap of cartoned bones
in the jaws of the poppy head.
we'll share no wish with
the down and out.

We are safe as the gloved hand
of the charity tin
the flushed colour of h appy wine
rosed upon our skin.

Hospital

The only colour is outside the room,
primary colours of spring to the nothing of the room.
Another sorry said.
This one feels heartfelt,
practiced in being said - a hundred times before
god knows
how many times today.

You are talking
we are listening, you are both talking
and listening.

On the nurse's desk there are waves of papers,
lapping at the dark blue jacket
of your medical notes,
shifting with the conversation.
Forms, templates, photocopies
a thousand times distant from the original
black lines of tick boxes of margin lines,
headings are lost
to a mist like evaporation, the fibered hairs
of cheap paper
a fog coming in.

You are talking
we are listening, you are both talking
and listening.
I am holding your hand like the blind.

I watched each face

coming into the waiting room;
young women alone
You don't know it yet
but how brave you will be.
For the couples who came in, the world
hangs around the torsos of the mothers;
either colour in their cheeks, full hair
or colour in their eyes, behind
the steady margin line
of black eye liner,
defiant to their grief,
a bet to themselves,

either way, good news or bad,
behind every new father's eyes
there's a frightened little boy.

I catch the eye of a boy and his reason
looks at me – too older than I should be
for sitting here? unfit for fatherhood,
a kick around a the yard,
to be that jack of all trades?
I have no wisdom for sitting here.
The colour outside is becoming a mosaic.
A plan is discussed,
agreed,
nodded too by me.

A blister pack and time is handed to you.

The first step in becoming one,
from us.

Nick Cirkovic

The Children in the Woods

Already he is racing away from me, the whir of the wheel along the zipwire speeding him beyond my reach. I am forgotten, left behind in the wake of his adrenalin rush, the wire scoring a diagonal, deep down into the vanishing point of the mulch-strewn slope.
"Pedal! Pedal!" The instructor shouts at him. "Like you're on your bike!" Ben doesn't hear: strung on the harness, legs dangling, swivelling at breakneck speed, twisting away form the point of impact, his body coming to rest at the line's termination with a silent hard slap onto his back, rusty rubber chippings flying. He lies there. I am breathless. He does not move.
"Quite a heavy landing your lad took there," the instructor mutters, a lick of a smile in his voice.
Ben gets up, dusts himself down and leads his harness line like the reins of an invisible horse to the point at which he disengages it from the trail runner, scrambles back excitedly to the tree top arena, his laughter and chatter with Rosa echoing through the colonnade of trunks.
And in the trees, beyond where he had fallen hard, dusty motes tumbling upon the air, there is a powdery green film of moss on the barks. Something moves between them. As I work my way along the platform to its edge, a simulacrum of a face is thrusting forward from the scaly trunk bole, distended features, drooping eye sockets, a motionless melt into sorrow and shadow. It moves again.
"Come on Daddy!"
Thick bands of gun grey metal bind the tree trunks where the harness wheel runners are secured, fleshy shavings of fibrous orange bark lining their rim like an open wound. I don't want to leave the safety of the trunk platform, to lunge off the edge along the zipwire. My mind is playing the slow motion flawed metal decay, the cracking of the hook lock holding me in my harness to the zipwire; my body

a sack of shit plunging in terminal freefall to the ground. I step forward, haplessly measuring my physical manhood against the instructor's devil-may-care demeanour on the edge of the platform.

"Your turn next!"

In the grip of vertigo my mind is manifesting monstrosities. The trajectory at which I hit the ground, body leant back, legs at an awkward angle – means on impact when my harness suffers its freak break, I hit the ground so hard, so wrong, my femur joints shoot out of my pelvic bone. I see it: the round ball of the femur joint, the shiny, fatty orb of it, bloody knob of shattered bone through ripped flesh. Among all the people coming and going, over all of the days, weeks, months and years in this place – a fatal accident is a statistical certainty sooner or later. I hesitate to move – forward. Move forward. There are children behind me, catching me up now – I am ashamed. Grown man, father, *Daddy*, hunched over, clinging for dear life to the harness chord attaching me to the wire run across the treetops.

I knew at the first obstacle that as soon as my foot touched the X-marks-the-spot daisy chain line of planking, my footfall would become as insubstantial as shifting cloud, each swinging X suspended by four ropes at its corners, forcing me to do the splits, expose me to the abyss beneath me, a ridiculous manifestation without, for all to witness, of my fear within. Harness or no harness, stretching out up here beyond the dignity of normal physical stability is not my idea of fun. I am grateful for the solidity of the platform now. Two boys behind me are plunging toward the platform across from the V-net, batting through the netting like it is nothing but limp creepers in their way, foolishly fearless. Just a child's tree-top activity adventure, for God's sake. I look down again, brain reeling, belly roiling.

"Ready?" The instructor asks and *I am not*. My memory of the lame asides I offered to the two girl instructors fitting my harness at the start of the climb down below, feeling my groin ache agreeably while they fussed and fitted my kit around my thighs comes back up at me. They *were* laughing, because they were embarrassed for you. Knowing a fall from this height can kill me, I plunge off the platform anyway, embarrassment triumphing over fear, slave to that racing whirr of the harness line along the down swoop of the zipwire. Exhilaration hits me full frontal, ground flying toward me. Faces – wax-melts in my rush past – watch me from below. Fighting to face forward, hitting the ground feet first I remain upright upon the sinking rubbery pathway of a dream. Pleased with myself, I am facing the vanishing point of the woods from Ben's trajectory only moments before, tree trunk and bark; a leaf canvas of composite, oval and hand shapes. Something moves. Wood snaps, cracks the air asunder. A distant quad bike saws into silence.

Beside a gall-bulged trunk the boy stands silent, arms motionless by his sides, hair a loose jagged straw stack atop his skull, his dumb lips parted, two glistening strawberry slugs. Head hung askew, his blue eyes stare at me in recognition; stare through me, looking forgotten in the woods, trying to remember. I have to angle my body round to get the harness wire free upon the runner, head craning over my shoulder. Looking and knowing I have imagined him through the trees. There are so many children, so much movement, so many bodies, so many projectiles of noise, shouts, laughter, gasps, ricocheting through the pillars of wood, that he is easily lost among them, carried away by an excited group of adults and other children.

Where is Ben? I spy him ahead, without a care, his chunky little legs scuttling off. By the time I am at the second set of stairs, leading up into the second trail of the two tree top routes, there is another pair of children between him and me.

In my fitful progress I imagine impatient climbers worrying at my shoulder, making faces, spitting mockery from out of the sides of their mouths. I look back to see a little girl standing sullen and motionless. Her long pale hair, off-blonde and dull grey slivers, hanging either side of her thin face; her pale lips drooping from hour upon practised hour of impassive silence. She is staring up at me with grey, unblinking orbs, glassy dilations, her features an unplaced twin for my memory. The harness webbing hangs limp upon her. The sun glaring at the corner of my eye and the faux fade of her pink hoodie top only bleach further the pallor of her complexion, accentuating the big strawberry birthmark standing out on her forehead.

The energy her mother exudes drains the life of everyone else around her. Her too tight black jeans clinging to her thighs, the harness webbing bulging them like bondage gear; her too low-cut white blouse clinging from her breasts, her own bright pink hoodie unzipped down to her fat black leather belt cinched waist, a pair of brilliant white and red flash Converse trainers looking brand new on those too small feet, tasked with buttressing and balancing the bold body display they are supporting above. One thick violet-veined ankle is decorated by a thin gold chain with a small heart locket dangling. Long black lashes flashing all about her, revealing bruise-blushed blue lids between thick tan foundation. Her perfume overpowering in its artificial bubble gum injection. She tugs and paws from behind without touching, gesturing with her man toward her daughter's doll-like submission always just beyond her grasp. The girl's stare does not waver. A stare that knows who I am, knows my darkest thoughts. Here's one for you: *Stop staring you little brat.* The little girl looks up at me and licks her lips with a hungry smile. I hurry back up into the trees.

At the top of the stairs leading onto the next platform I bow my head, pause for another breath. I lift my nose up, tracing a familiarly pleasant aroma in the air, sweet, sticky, the wet strawberry and apple of a licked lollipop. Clara's sweetness lingers. In her lilac-patterned pumps she is leaping from plank to plank like a gazelle, flowery, balmy, gasping a happy laugh like the children in her care. I stand still amid the sensation, amid the bright, momentary calm of this April afternoon, caught in its scent, her scent; a mother's scent of sweets and wipes, of cotton linen laundry conditioner and the balmy perfume of our night before; every attribute just as real and desirable in her as the ache the coarse, Converse, come-on bubble gum mess now thumping up toward me has just put down there. A vague flutter of a breeze through the branches is the rattle of old bones. *Bones on the breeze, blood in the stream.* The planking trembles under my feet like a shudder of conscience.

Above the gaps in the canopy, scuds of whiter cloud are pushed away by great weighty darker gluts, sliding the whole surface of the sky along with them. I would rather this looking up than looking down. But looking along is what I must do now, look along, at any moment sucked down into the whirlpool of my vertigo, a hovering turmoil beneath me.

Behind me, the mother of the sullen little girl is playing up the experience for all it is worth, with her pub laugh and exaggerated exclamations of "Oh-my-god!" Intermittent screams accompany her aped ineptitude and exhibitionist helplessness. It violates the greenery, chased after by the raucous animal joy of the flung-headed laughter that follows each fantastical bird-like shriek. The ache dulls and I understand the vow of silence her daughter's sullen presence is holding.

The second trail runs higher than the first, akin in torment to the walkways beneath it, but this one, as its showpiece, forces me to ascend a spiralling stepped platform round the trunk, adding a further ten feet to my ordeal. Here the distance between the first trunk platform and the second consists of two tightropes, the second at chest height with enough slack to cause involuntary judders, the entire body lurching back, lurching forward to play what-shall-we-do-with-the-drunken-sailor in mid-air. Shouting, chattering, skittering birds, laughter, a scream stabbing through it all and the intense inner silence of my body's sweeping back and forth, waving its semaphore of help and alarm and the imminence of danger. A voice inside tells me to have a word with myself, all the while I am gripping the contact point between my harness wheel and the lead wire runner; exactly what I have been told not to do. I slide my grip further down the harness line. With my grip no longer along on the harness wire wheel running over the wire the instability becomes intensified. Bastards. But I leave it there, further down, visions of a finger trapped and crushed between wheel and wire if I move it up again, wondering why it hasn't happened already.

Samson is in difficulty. Ben has always been a blundering boldness in the playground beside his hesitant school friend. I look below and see Samson poised, shivering on the planking, refusing to budge, locked tight within the sheer determination of his fear. There are coaxes and cajolings, to my pride Ben is also cheer-leading Samson on, shouting out team-building moral boosters along with everyone else; willing Samson to press on. Samson remains adamant in his halted movement, flinching from their calls like cast stones. Something is shouted out, all calling ceases. An instructor is taking charge, climbing up to the platform, circumventing the group in between Samson and himself. He is standing behind Samson now, marshalling him forward step by step across the line of parallel planking, arms about the rescued little one, soft-toned, affirmative, all action-webbed wonder man. He takes the weeping Samson off the tree tops altogether and I am a glad dad that I don't have to deal with the fallout from the likes of that. Samson is down on *terra firma* now, sobbing or not – the lucky little bugger.

Looking across the thoroughfare that cuts through the a mass of trees, one tree, in its huge squat bulkiness – a chestnut maybe – stands solitary to the left of the main mass. I am caught unaware, the sun blasting through a passing cloud, exposing the finer veins and the charcoal skeleton of the tree's entire structure. I shield my eyes from the glare until the fuse of light, two stark whites in my corneas, evaporates. A lone wood pigeon clings to a branch up top, swaying in the breeze, beak tucked into its breast, feathers ruffled; thin and raggedy up there, clinging on. Clumped on the branches that are nodding and flapping, the leaves are fluttering their silent incessant chatter of a thousand tongues against the sky. Behind, they are catching up with me.

These extra ten feet make all the difference. Before, I can face the physical possibility of hanging full length from the tightrope by my hands if I have to, to reassure myself that I am not that high, dropping back to the ground, nothing but a turned ankle to show for it. Now, as I look down – don't look down, *do-not-look-down* – I am in femur-shooting territory.

The climb began in cool air, my body experiencing a slight chill, now it has grown uncomfortably warm. With no idea what to expect for this children's party treat – *You never listen*, Clara will tell me – I haven't come dressed for any of it. Other dads of invited children are wearing their mid-thirties and middle-aged nods to trendy I'll-have-a-go sport and leisure gear. I can feel the pits of my arms beginning to dampen, my long-sleeved shirt hangs sloppily out of my jeans, the harness webbing has rutched them up and is digging disagreeably into my groin. Amid the trampled greenery and the dusty grey surface of the woodland floor below, a bright straw dot brings me to a full stop. The little boy is looking up, head still askew, the bright red O of his strawberry slugs for lips now a thin flat-lined purple, those blue eyes ever vacant, a stare of mindless awe up at and through me. The lips begin to turn at the corners. The boy turns his face away from me before I hear Ben scream across the treetops and snap my head round following the boy's prescient gaze. My eyes are a panicked search for Ben's bright blue training top, his scarlet sweat pants. I hear his unbridled laughter before I see him, hurtling to safety along the zipwire line. The little boy below me is gone.

Another raucous shriek over my shoulder and I look now in sympathy for the sullen girl trailing the two children who follow behind me. Gone. The woman remains and with her, her stevedore partner, arms wrought with tattooed sigils, swelling through a marl grey T-shirt printed with illiterate bullshit about Executive Winning Gym 1958 Santa Monica Team Cap. His blue wode muscles goosing her round the waist, she is whooping delight over her shoulder at him; his shaven head an ash blond bullet butting her neck in their bolting horseplay.

My body bucks involuntarily, I lurch forward, doubling over – the wire snapping me back again.

"Two at a time! Only two at a time!" I yell like a short-tempered school master at the two boys behind me on the wire. The boy in front steps back onto the tree trunk platform. Naughty schoolboy snickering. The hair of the boy behind looks matted, sodden, his face unhappy with me. He does not move. I look down, uncertain of the movement of heads beneath me on the woodland floor. I must press on to the safety of the next trunk platform, the man and woman already bursting impatiently behind the two boys.

"It's just like that place in *Lord of the Rings*," I can hear Rosa telling Ben, her voice ringing up toward me. No it is not.

"I haven't seen that, my daddy says…" Their incessant chatter is lost in the pell-mell of group noise and a stiffening breeze through the creaking branches. I look down and watch them trotting back to the first set of stairs again at the treetop adventure's starting point, nattering merrily away. Ben does not look up. I want to call out his name but I do not. He is far away. Ache of regret, the sharp stab of it in the chest…. "… I'm too young."

I want to be done with the tightrope, done with yet another acute V-shaped suspension of netting ahead, to be back down again to the level of sprained ankles. In my undignified flapping I am a trapped fly in a web. Body stooping over I attain the platform and gulp a lungful of relief, belly crunched, bulging over my belt buckle, my backside sticking out. Through the lines of trees and lower spread of fluttering leaves, lime, dull grey and racing green, muddy cream hand spans upon the branches, motionless beneath their wavering shadows: straw dots for head tops pepper the woodland floor. Under them, blank surfaces, stock still, staring up at me, each one a crash test dummy, a tabula rasa upon which to write my own fear-filled expressions. As one they turn and gaze away. Following their gaze I am caught suddenly at the sight of Ben, swinging like an ill-coordinated chimp from the harness line, unable to gain his footing again, the parallel planking that is swaying beneath him like a rogue hoverboard. I cannot help him, he is beyond my reach. Far away.

Each demanding gaze the children make comes as a warning: that instant gut-wrenching flood of fear when we lost him in the crowd for the minute that lasted for hours along the curving pathways of Legoland. He is still hanging and they are still here, I feel their mute stare upon him, awed, anticipatory. *Come into our arms. Rest beneath our limbs.*

I am in a panic to get down, to get him down. It will cause a scene, a scandal, Clara will be furious with me, the men will laugh; the mothers I see seldom and have sought to impress anew will laugh at me, their embarrassed looks like glancing blows below the level of my midriff. *They will always remember you this way.* The fear of ridicule overrides my fear for him. I do not move.

He is no longer dangling. With Rosa's help and pointy instructions affirmed by his keen exclamations of "Yeah, yeah," at his mastery of yet another new experience in life, he is moving on. A figure flits past my left shoulder and this cannot be. I turn, look about me. Gone. Only the smirking schoolboy at the end of the line. Below me upon the fading woodland carpet of greys and greens, a group of day out adventurers in yellows and pinks, peach and purples and the distinctive blue and red webbing of a Spider-man baseball cap cut a noisy swathe. I am forgotten up here.

From the moment we made the turn into the woodland car park there has been something different about today. New surroundings, a new experience, the quirky novelty of a birthday party adventure in the trees for 'Ninja Monkeys'. The first real day of spring after the grimness and rainy grime of a prolonged London winter. Something else. The wood is alive with families, children, café staff, instructors, laughter, shadows, colour and movement. The wood is alive.

From where I stand now within the treetop arena I can see the row of poplars that were a bold signpost on the approach to the car park, standing tall above the thick cluster of treetops between them and me. Angled back, yet defiantly upright in the face of the breeze, four forbidding sentinels standing in profile, high foreheads and tapering headdresses of upper branches, at one end one of them smaller, buckled at the top; a greenery of inscrutable Easter Island statues in the heart of Essex.

Swivelling awkwardly upon the harness in my imaginary safe zone of one square foot upon a good three yards' square platform, I graze my forehead against bark rough as stone, draw my index finger across my damp hair, flinch at the sudden wetness of let blood, to inspect only a lick of perspiration along the finger's edge. Standing there, harness line taught and squeaking, a mustiness lingers about me, coming off the old tree – the thrill of solitude I felt as a child rushing up in me, alone on the swings over the Dumps, alone when all the other children are tumbling back toward the estate, shoving, dawdling, nattering. They are calling out to me to join them while I tarry here; solitude has its thrilling, sensual hold upon me. They are calling out, bating me to follow while I remain upon the swing, rocking gently back and forth, legs dangling, watching them cutting a diagonal across the field, through the four big grass-skinned mounds of the Dumps, past the musty old oak we use as a goalpost – its thick flaky bark there to bash defenders' brains, to flay sliding strikers' knees and diving goalies' knuckles, amid volleys of random ricochets – disappearing into the alleyway. Among our gang I see Gary Ewins, sinking under halfway into the 100 metres crawl during the school swimming contest, hand up, hollering comically for help in the water, drowned in the Falklands War. There is Mark Davis, the school's blonde-haired, blue-eyed heartthrob. Everything to play for they said, in his mid-twenties – a good decade after I'd lost all contact with him, engaged to a lovely girl they said – having won and cast aside so lightly the helpless heart of Belinda Collins, the first true unrequited love of my life in Year 10 – who only a week before his wedding hung himself in his parents' loft one lunch hour home from work. There is pale-eyed Caitlin McCarthy, always blundering about boldly, long, lank hair swaying, without a care, killed outright head on by a Ford Cortina when she ran out onto the traffic right outside her house on the Oxford Road. We hear the scream of the breaking car wheels and the screams of her larger-than-life mum

Clodagh, we nicknamed 'Clodhopper' with perfunctory kids' cruelty – "My baby! My baby!" – from over the rooftops on the other side of the houses we hear it, where we stand in shock within the estate's no longer safe embrace. As I look out across the open space beyond the tree climb arena, an arc of closely packed trees are forming a perimeter, the colours of the children in the woods are livid now against the greys and pale greens and browns of the tree bark. *Come. Come.* The children as solid as the trunks they stand beside, behind, in between, gazing.

The birthday partygoers' laughter is a world away from me. Forgotten up here I am my own independent eco-system of horrors. The children are coming closer now. S*mall down-in-the-dumps boy on the swing. Come.* So make it stop. Make it stop. Come. You can make it stop. Move. But I do not. I cannot. *These arms we will break.* Every step Ben takes without me, oblivious of the fret and love and worry to come, is a terror to me. *Come. Come.* Every leap Clara makes, every laugh without me as sad and heavy and insubstantial in me as the clouds drifting above. *These limbs we will take.* Not today. Not today. *One day*. Not yet. *One day. One day.* Not for a long time yet. Not for a lifetime yet.

Now I move, step once again off the platform onto the zipwire run, "Wait!" the instructor cries. Foolishly brave, I do not. The grinding crack of the zipwire wheel runner, the rip of the harness webbing is like broken bone and torn flesh through my body. I hang heavy and speechless, swinging helplessly upon the wire, hand waving for something to hold, the screams shrieking over the treetops echoed back by the birds' fantastical cries.

"Daddy! Daddy!"

The children are facing up at me from the woodland floor, mouths gaping, silent and hungry, eyes wide and unseeing. The jolt of the breaking harness snaps my dead weight upside down and I fall head-on now – an exhilarating, terrifying rush of blood to the brain in my freefall down, down into their empty, outstretched, waiting arms.

Claire Scott

My Grandmother's Purse

A wrinkled red bag with lots of zippers and snaps
    and striped peppermints in the outside pocket
    wrapped in crinkly cellophane
lotion smelling of sweet oranges rubbed
    on my hands after rambling walks
    in Central Park, boots sloshing wet snow
a coin purse with quarters for oatmeal raison
    cookies at *Sweet Dreams*
    pennies for gum balls at *Safeway*
gobs of keys on a key chain with my first grade picture
    gap toothed grin
    uncombed hair
pens with red ink, blue ink, green ink, purple ink
and a pad so I can scrunch on the floor and draw
    pictures of a child alone
    cradling her Paddington bear
while my grandmother waits in line at the bank
    greeting each teller by name
    Hello Francie, Hi Dustin
a packet of Kleenex for tears
Arnica for slaps and bruises
sometimes a trinket or two
    a game of jacks, a silver ring,
    a necklace with a shiny cross
    she says will keep me safe

Actually just a plain leather bag
with two vials of pills, a single key
a lipstick I am not allowed to touch
a jumble of wadded tissues

Actually no cookies, no gum balls, no jacks
only hurry up, stand straight, tie your shoes
time to take you home
words I dread to hear

Dirty Hands

My older brother Mr. Perfect always did his homework, read chapter books for extra credit, won all the spelling bees. He spelled *impeccable* and *unimpeachable*. I hated him. At night he set the table without being asked, washed the dishes, emptied the garbage. I sulked in the corner, ignoring my schoolwork, drawing stick figures of my brother and X-ing them black. He never balked at going to Sunday school where we cut out dumb Jesus's and stupid Mary's and pasted them on construction paper. I try to be nice, really I do most of the time. But you need to know this. When I was six my mother hung starched sheets on the clothes line, billowing clouds of perfection. I ran among the sheets dragging muddy hands, wild dancing in the morning sun before putting hand prints all over my brother's third grade science project. I like to think I have gotten past this pettiness, but some days I want to straggle filthy fingers down the front of his all-too-white button down shirt.

HI HO SILVER!

A game of pretend I played when I was six or seven and we had just gotten the tiniest ever black and white TV. Three channels. I watched the Lone Ranger on Saturdays at noon. I couldn't wait for *A fiery horse with the speed of light a cloud of dust and a hearty Hi Ho Silver!* I loved his white horse, his silver bullets and the mystery of the black mask. Every week he defeated the bad guys in less than half an hour. Every episode ended with *Hi Ho Silver, Away!* Galloping up to the same exact rock where week after week Silver rears up on hind legs. Predictable. Comforting. Unlike the chaos of my home where meals were random and often burnt. Where I could hear glass shattering, screams of *I hate you! stupid bitch! shut up!* Hiding in my room, I turned on an imaginary TV and switched to the future channel. I played this game again and again. Each time, all I saw was the dull fuzz of snow. The way the TV looked at night when the programming ended. I never told anyone. Until years later, as I lay on my therapist's couch, I spoke in stuttered sentences. She looked at me with a face full of sorrow. *You were depressed she said.* I cried for the child who had no future. The child who couldn't gallop away on a white horse. I fingered the silver bullet in my pocket.

Your Neighbour

> *It is a disaster to discover the humanity of your enemy.*
> —Colum McCann

His relatives take up all the parking spaces with their rusted out trucks. It is impossible to convince him to keep his dog off your lawn since he is barely civil, smokes cigars, cooks stinky cabbage, speaks with an accent, has a bushy beard, no doubt from one of the Stans, maybe Kazakhstan, a disaster waiting to happen. Tomorrow you will buy rat poison. You pray he will move to Australia. Then this morning as you were leaving late as usual you discover your daughter riding a pink bike brrring-brrringing a bell down the hill, the bike his daughter used to ride pony tail flying. Faced with his in-your-face humanity your anger deflates like a two day old mylar balloon leaving only a pale rind of memory, no tight stomach, no clenched teeth, no fist of rage to support your fury. You lie listless on your bed, totally bereft without your belovèd enemy.

Professional Worrier

Yesterday it was rogue waves slapping across our lawn sweeping away our house our Honda our cat Bailey who is past due for a rabies shot probably too late perhaps partially paralyzed is that foam in his mouth does our insurance even cover rogue waves do they ever answer their phone where will we live certainly not with our daughter who eats only vegan disgusting green piles of puréed vegetables for sure malnutrition rickets or beriberi impossible to cure definitely Lyme disease since she lives in the country well not exactly the country more like in West Philadelphia where there are poisonous spiders black widows bringing muscle cramps nausea suddenly-sudden death far away from our swept-away-by-a-rogue-wave home in Omaha, Nebraska

Delphi Once Removed

a sure sign:
two calico cats cross the street at 2:02
then wander off in different directions

a definitive message
to leave my husband *toute de suite*
off to Paris with Marceau who I met last week

with his gold rings & private plane
a bit older, maybe twenty years, no, tell it right: thirty
a few inches shorter, definitely rounder
but *o la la* he owns an oil rig off the coast of Louisiana
& speaks French with a French accent

what I do know is this
Oedipus killed his father & married his mother
no possible way to avoid his destiny
follow the oracle, go with the flow
& right now I am flowing, baby, I am flowing

all packed for Paris
four suitcases stuffed with couture clothes
& Jimmy Choo shoes
charged to my soon-to-be-ex's Master Card
but where the hell is Marceau?

Little One

I hold your tiny hand
and worries toss my head
spiral through my heart
you not eating
barely breathing
I will roll over you
as I dream of earthquakes
tsunamis and cyclones
you will slip from my soapy
hands and shatter
only two weeks old
and I worry
you will choke on your pacifier
fall from a slide
cross the street without looking
I worry
there will be no telltale click
to say you are home
just past midnight
I touch your face
feel your soft skin
little one let my fears fly by
like angel dust or feathers
drifting in a morning breeze

Annie McCrea

A Poor Girl's Rehab

she is transferred from an ambulance and
waits outside the consulting room. They've sent
someone junior to do the deal
a psych in suit and tie. He says "Now here
is the deal, this section's for real." The doc
checks for signs of delusion and she goes high.

reeling in rests of collateral damages, she
revokes diagnoses of nervous collapses.
air brushed from eternity are signs of time's ravages
a camera pans in never ending synapses
the Low heeled high boot boys strike incandescent poses
no Oscar for her just one techni colour minute
the credits roll to the tune of sidereal roses
the psych shakes his head and says
you'll be here a while.

This cameo role is in her head not on screen
One moment of fame in a psychotic dream.

Rain in summer

not April showers but summer
unannounced so that you
get caught
without a raincoat

frizzy hair shaking your head
seeking shelter in cafes loving
summer but smelling autumn.

Judith Hearne is alive and well

on the corner of Camden street
it was on one of these streets
that my Victorian grandfather
whose most usual saying
was Bounce and thirteen children
separately or together bounced
to attention came to die in a nursing home in
Camden street
she could not have known
that years on
his granddaughter would play
super ball in the back yard
and thinking of her grandfather
bounce the ball high as a skylark
while downtown Bobby Vee
sang Rubber Ball

A name for that

am so in tune with nature
I could whistle Ode to Joy
and lift both feet off
the ground in a sideways jump
there has to be a name for that

i'm wondering at the Sugar Loaf
peppered with snow like a Paris bun
there has to be a name for that i'm
feeling as irrepressible
as a jack-in-the box
as high as the mountains
which tomorrow I'll climb
there should be a name for that

i'm blowing hot and cold
like the wind that skims
through the firs on the hills
above Glendalough
there should be a name for that

i'm listening to Beatrice
humming Amazing Grace
downstairs in the kitchen
why can't I find a name for that?

Break-up

the way an old dressing gown
draped around a chair
in graffiti which sped
by from a train window
symptoms of a malaise
and an affair which floundered

her lover now incommunicado
she learnt to exist in a limbo
of cyphers
. -,/!;#=;//
peppering the horizon
and conspiring against
their meeting of minds
like empty speech bubbles
cast across the Irish sea

Bruce Bromley

Heart Hurt

Tell me we'll never get used to it.
Richard Siken, 2005

The boy didn't know what to do with sounds that entered his head and became something else. His parents would soon be caught in the glare of their weekly murder mystery, its theme a barrage of horns lingering too long on the tonic, the note of houses and pillows and safe spaces, before charging up a diminished fifth and arriving at the tritone, or what his music teacher called "our satanic interval": it bedeviled the consonance that any ear ached for, whose achievement told the body where it was. Moments earlier, the boy had listened to the square of front lawn between his bedroom and the den, where his parents made themselves into the drinks they couldn't let go of and were about to merge with a televised disaster story they'd survive. He'd heard a mockingbird stump through the grass, part its beak on an E that rang across the air, that slid down a major third and up one step, a mating call hovered over by the moon, incapable of calling back. The boy saw these notes dotted on a staff as if he weren't in bed but floating high above them, the mockingbird's tune overlaid with booming horns in a gob of scored pitches he didn't know how to disentangle. He thought of his younger brother coiling in a tight S on the other side of the oval rug that separated them, how sleep was his hunger for the womb that made him. The boy thought of his own head pulped by sound becoming sight. And then he watched an archway rise up from the floor between their beds, its white like wobbling smoke through which he found another place, its details failing to come clear. He tugged the covers over him and was on his belly when the touch came, a triplet of touches on his lower spine, made by what he'd never identify as a hand. In the morning, sitting up, he looked down at the once shelved books he shared with his brother flopped in a mound on the rug you couldn't see, clothes off their hangers and encircling them. This room, the boy knew, was in the middle of a turn into something else, when the turning stopped.

At 36, he was still a boy because the nurses called him one. He thought of his generation's interest in contracting itself in terms of time, so that everyone was a boy, a girl, who couldn't be permitted to grow up, since aging resisted the will to control it and ended in a process that no one had words for, as you wouldn't be there to say them. He remembered Raymond Burr, the defense attorney and lead in the series of horror tales that ended well, weekly, through which his parents medicated themselves, along with much else, against the mess of feeling too much. Burr was big and wide, though his walk belonged to a smaller man judging the range of space he meant to cross. He lived in a California where people were always disappearing and defended the right person blamed for the wrong crime, a skill that each episode patterned. Burr would challenge one of the prosecution's witnesses when something inside him began to glow, a luster whose signal said: you caused the lethal disappearance of which my client must be innocent. And that was a man's picture in the early-to-mid 1960s, at least within the frame of a tube television set, this becoming aglow that lit up what had been wrongly obscured. The boy tried to focus on his doctor, holding a group of X-rays in the light that shimmied off the East River, beyond his isolation room's window. These were the arches of his lungs, their tissue opalescent, polyped by a virus that would remain unseen. He imagined wings evolving over all of it, long bones feathered a pollinating green in a gesture towards flight and fertility, elsewhere. But that internal, that future flight was what he had no name for. A first person pronoun in the midst of vanishing, how does it speak? The words might sound like:

– I'm in a world where men are called boys and vaporize at a pace brisker than the time needed to recognize that they were there. It's 1993, 12 years after the initial reports of GRID gave way to being reborn as AIDS, and I'm in New York Hospital's emergency room, sitting on a revolving chair whose wheels won't turn, forcing my attention on an admitting nurse, her name unknown, ungiven to me, who stretches up like the snow-encrusted city outside, a place gone cold blue. She's busy with telling me what I am, on the basis of her decrypting the X-rays I've brought with me, as if—together—they were a passport to some other country. I've cabbed them here from my doctor's office, a man who asks me to call him "Charlie" and who became a widower last month, when Charlotte, the wife whose face he cupped in his hands for 50 years, disappeared from the sheets she'd no longer get up from, though her body made their bed a heated plate and lay there, beside him. That's the whole of it, Charlie said, or the whole he could bear to carry: death was a blazing—until it wasn't. I'd come to him a week ago with a hacking that wouldn't quiet. It began a month earlier, in December, when my father and I were shying from waves on that East Hampton beach where our family-dead used to drink and swim and lunch and wrangle at love on the dunes, braving ticks. They seemed to bristle around us as each wave stood up, refusing the air and its ice. I was on a break from working on my second undergraduate degree. My first, in music, wouldn't bring me into classrooms where I'd think through essays with students who didn't yet know the strain that widens what you can't believe you are. I returned to the country I never knew how to live in after making music across Europe for all of the 1980s, followed by men whose wives, girlfriends, and mothers were uninformed that I was there. Arriving at Columbia University, I sped myself up in a crowd of words and books and essays, forgetting the body's need, sometimes, to stop. I'm on a broken chair, listening to a nurse with ice-chips in her eyes: you're a gay man with an opportunistic infection. The X-rays indicate it's a pneumonia, associated only with AIDS patients. So, you're dying. I'm admitted into a many windowed isolation room. Doctors wrestle behind their masks with the contradiction between what they term my clinical presentation—more brightly colored than it should be—and their diagnosis, even after multiply testing negative for the disease they insist I can't survive. I won't be made into the man who's called a boy by nurses, undone by a syllogism, by this reasoning together of a body, its inclinations, and their aftermath. But I don't know if denial is how the disappearing starts.

– I'd known disappearance before, as an experience of almost being halved. In Paris, for a while I lived behind a gas station on the quai d'Austerlitz, half of a two-part franchise run by Chanh. He'd studied philosophy at the Sorbonne yet upheld his native Laos in the alternating chop and sinuousness of his vowels, in the mint leaves he draped over steamed rice. But his love of wisdom sharpened his sense that the daughter of the judge he hoped to marry would reject him, that her family must wince at his feasibility. In the business of curtailing his capacity to rise, the State would grant him citizenship, the right to supervise two Left Bank stations, and remove them from him when it suited. He heard that give-and-take in how his customers wondered at the easy music of his French, as if the brief stoop down to notice him made them, somehow, taller. Chanh offered me the apartment in the rear of his station on the quai because, years ago, he'd worked the reception desk at a Montmartre hotel: meeting the newlyweds of my sister and her husband, together they rhapsodized over the city that gave them room. Now, halfway through 1983, on a night when fog circled street lamps like breath made visible, we were celebrating summer's start. Chanh's French "guy friends," as he called them, gifted with loans they'd lose sight of repaying, overfilled our glasses with *eau de vie* they drove back from the South and its heat. I was walking to the gas station's mean cell of a toilet, pulling the door to, when the tiled floor seemed to hump up and hit me above the right eye. And suddenly I was a kind of two: a heap of flattened limbs and this male body watching the boundaries between things judder, in a frequency hop and overlap that he—or I—could see. In one long quiver, I found my sister with her new son in his Brooklyn bedroom, a tree twisting on the other side of the window, urban, lost at the center of the building's geometry in what kindness would call a courtyard. She combed the boy's scanty hair while dusk grew around them and didn't know why her husband came back, each day, so late. In a tremble, I stood inside the doorway of my mother's bedroom when East Hampton air made a sort of salty mist over her dressing table. She looked in a mirror for the face that had said "yes" to my father, not knowing if its force still held. And, a vertical line tautening above that body on the floor of a gas station's toilet, I became this hand touching the blood on my forehead. Landing in one body at a single moment: was it really just another way to leave?

– My hospital room's peopled with loved ones who try to keep me from the departure they fear. At 110, 20 pounds have veered from me. More will follow them. The unproductive gag of my cough has gone mute, thanks to what my medical team pumps through the IV I'm married to. Tom and Amanda, friends from Columbia, flank the side rails of my bed and tell me about an *out there* I can't imagine reaching. Tom's got a mini player with him. He arranges it on my bedside table, hands me a wrapped CD set, whose mechanics I'm not up to managing. Their coupledom's a pageant I don't know how to join, in a future set of possibilities that won't be mine. I'm told how my life will return to its track, that I can be whatever I want to be, but I'm not a train, not a homily, and this likening of experience to what it's not must be a sleep that any life should refuse to settle into. When my father, mother, sister, and brother leave for the day, I zoom in on some distinction between getting used to dying and being in it. I'm out of bed, my IV-husband straggling behind me. The window yields a river so lushly blue that it's a crime to blink before it. I'll stand in what my body gives me and acknowledge that none of us can predict how long the staying lasts.

— My doctors flag me with being immunosuppressed. They worry it's invited in the double pneumonia making a tumble of my lungs, even as I continue to test negative for the AIDS they now doubt I have. But suppression and tumbling have a backstory, and I think of it as a wasting of my kind. Gay, lesbian, transgender: we inhabit a country whose history has wanted us gone, and sometimes we help with the going. That's a skill set we can learn, faced with many who wish we weren't here, who teach us to take the power to waste and aim it at what will effect that work. As a teenager, I danced in a company organized by Leila Katayen and Val Telberg, who smuggled their lives out of the Soviet Union to perform a marriage of movement and photography that their country was determined to disallow. Val would point his camera at dune grass in a storm of wind, a blue scarf airborne over sand and project their images on each company-member. Leila dressed us in semi-transparent sacks, urging on the sharp rise and downward push of every limb, in time to electronic music by Alwin Nikolais, its abrupt tones and silences answered by a flare of chords in the hope that one expressive medium was transforming into another. But inside my sack, as we toured the East Coast, I became the boy who liked too much the thinness that Leila praised, the grass and scarves that Val shot close up, transported to an elsewhere that the lens showed no interest in registering. Some transformations, I'd learn, had invisibility as their end. Kevin modeled clothes for Comme des Garçons: he'd starve for a week to make them his and talk about *this unseen verge*. On the edge of 1980, before I left for Europe, we danced in New York clubs that came and went once they got the fame their owners yearned for, whose achievement, Kevin insisted, made them cheap. So, they'd materialize somewhere else, reborn by another name. We were dancing under the revolving ball that spangled the crowd's heave to Prince's wail. We noticed how men we loved and some we didn't weren't coming back. I'm a black man in a life of always trying to stand up, Kevin said, but this virus and its changing names will have us all unseen, unfleshed, unmade. Our nation that doesn't care enough needs to hear those still standing speak about the waste.

– I'm listening to Tom's CD, replaying Arvo Pärt's *Trisagion*. Three-times holy: the Greek of Pärt's title belongs to the liturgy of the Eastern Orthodox Church, its practices a long look at the Estonian past that the Soviets worked at wiping out. They exiled Pärt from his homeland because he wouldn't craft music piping the wonders of the State. But he took Estonia with him in the lamentation of its intervals. The place drifts up and holds there, anchored by Pärt's fashioning of the old sounds, made new. The Greek may describe a holiness in triplicate, since God is holy, holy strong, holy never ending, yet the hymn closes with the imperative to have mercy on us, who qualify him. Pärt takes his string orchestra and puts it in a rhythm of three propulsive beats, their sequence repeated, the double basses and cellos, the violas and violins divided, so their widening registers leave a hollow between them. In that hollow, I think of the devotional burdens that Pärt's God must hold to, the taking care of each piece of matter on the earth he made. I'm thinking, ordered or not by a generative God, of how triple holiness ought to be directed at all earthly matter and must merit the mercy of being saved. I'm leaving my isolation room tomorrow, free of double pneumonia and that AIDS I never had, though carrying scarred lungs. Right now, I look at dusky water and feel a casement window hinging open in my chest. And every pore I've got sucks in the light that's left.

26 years after that exit from my hospital room, it's almost dawn. My partner, Neil, paints on the floor in our north-facing living room, his trowel and hands building up curls of mist over a blue rectangle, horizontally inclined in the middle distance. He watches for light he can get and remakes its pulsations on canvas. Among sheets, in our bedroom pointing south, I'm in a Brooklyn apartment on land where—in the 1630s—my father's Dutch ancestors ravaged the

bodies that preceded them, scratching at an older world in favor of the one they maintained was new. About that smoky archway ascending from the floor and almost open to some other place, about juddering, hopping between time zones and their variant locations: it comes to me that where we lie or stand or walk must be adjacent to where we think we're not. The lives we plot for ourselves or allow to be plotted for us, when anything else seems beyond imagining, interface with what many don't yet understand enough to entitle with a name. But otherness can be reached for, enacted in a single life's stretch, and it can spread. Raymond Burr outlasted the role of Perry Mason that made him, sustaining a lifetime of loving men in a country whose laws negated such loving. He performed the possibility that you can buck at jurisprudence when its operations mean to disorder you—and still stand up. Today, my doctorate long behind me and at New York University, where I've taught for 23 years my medical team pronounced I wouldn't live to see, students and I are going to concentrate on Audre Lorde. We'll listen to her directive that silence won't protect us. Any culture needs to be stretched by the speaking back committed to reordering it, rightly. I'm about to pull up bedroom blinds on this fragrant June green that hurts me around the heart, and I know I can never get used to it.

That's some of what surviving tells me.

Dorian Nightingale

Decrescendo II

in from the void an emergent sensation,
an unfolding vibration drifting through the air. a beckoning wave of
seamless sound beguiling the atmosphere.
floating to the opening heralding the finale,
the arrival of an Emperor awaking dormancy gently.

subdued fingers revived from solemn inactivity,
a fluttering embryonic fidget of a rejuvenated motivity. reimagined
conversancy stirred by a faraway remembrance,
a salvaged shard of consciousness coerced from death's
encumbrance.

a grand piano most perfectly reproduced,
an innermost expression by a corporeal ghost.
tapping fingers and striking hammer conjoined simultaneously,
invoking the latency of early childhood proficiency.

rekindled memories reciting present improvisation, contemplation of
the template without hesitation. invisible architecture for sweeping
articulation, an authentic claviature for stimulating imagination.

strings and woodwind chaperone the silent romance, dancing
melodic companions consorting the ambiance. glided hands
embrace the swoop of gilded harmonies as enlaced arpeggios stoop
to climb then decline to rise with ease contouring the hush and the
rush of acoustic variation, sculpting murmurations whittle and hew
the fluid fluctuation. shaping the phrases with emotive synchrony,
immersed in the moment an enrapturing symphony.

then winding down to a whispered resound, movement begins to diminish. recedent echoes withdrawing sound ushering in the finish.

disorganized, disharmonized, arms lag behind the tempo. in limbo limbs enervated, exhausted,
befallen to a shadow.

Unable to continue.

yet perched on a staff a cherished note, a motionless finger rests. indefinitely deceiving the final denouement, a forever defiant bequest.

Decrescendo V

gasping rasping breathing barely bearable wheezing squeezing
grasping air inhaling now intolerable deairing chest deflating
fast speedily incapable tormented obsessed unrested respiration
desperate deprivation suffocation insufferable swiftly sinking
resisting shrinking submersing spirit submerging strength condition
getting serious drowning in air drowning despair drowsing
concentration cannot go on cannot continue to slip in situ this
expiring exertion reversion reduced to   a   sip asthmatically sick
engulfed by asphyxia de facto in absentia acutely aware of this
unaired nightmare an unchecked condition of choking attrition
dissolving resolve unsolving this toxic pulmonic no help alone no
sound unfound this unfainting fight unmedicated alight devoid of
respite passing in passing out fading in fading out failing fast rapidly
inoperable swallowing impossible cannot respire just aspiring to
keep breath and offset the onset of the fateful inevitable...

... then seeping through the dissipating awareness an imbuing hue
of enveloping darkness a developing black cloud of unknown
conception, an uncertain inception, disbanding senses
within expanding oblivion.

an encompassing blankness revoking resistancy, a serenity evoked
from the yoke of opacity. an acquiescing experience extricating
sentience, inducing obedience impassive subservience. sedation
seceding cognizant efficiency, conceding even respiratory
expediency.

breathing an unnecessary inconveniency.

feeling becomes unfeeling, sense becomes unsense. consciousness
gently dissolving unable to respond,
before stripping away that very conception back into the beyond.

meekly accepting irrational disposition,
weakly complying within the comfort of nothing.

blending in, becoming one,
witnessing the last vestiges of the self slowly melting running
down, grounded down becoming the absorbent blankness of
expressionless unconcerning

withdrawn now to a hiding place, undetected
but just alive.

an invisible foxhole as yet unrevealed, concealed encoiled inside.

waiting

lost in a refuge for last imaginations

Gret Heffernan

Artificial Intelligence

1995 in Laurel Canyon, she sliced open her finger with a bread knife, vomited at the sight of blood and knew you were with her. ER was full of actors and junkies. She wondered about him. So he took her speeding through the 2nd Street Tunnel. Blade Runner to prove a point. Night blur and the Bradbury Building, where he removed a Phillips from his shirt pocket and slowly tightened each of her screws. Because he had thought about where bolts would fit into her body, she let him.

"Reality exists inside the artificial," he'd say, meaning love. In bed, he liked to pretend to be Roy. "All these moments will be lost in time, like tears in rain. Time to die," he'd say and trace her. Months later, bits of you in the toilet. Little floating islands. There are worlds that end and begin on the space of a thumbprint. A clot of seaweed. Moss. You were wise not to stay. He died high on a motorcycle. Strange how humans will cherish what they're incapable of carrying, a portion of time. You'll learn to live like this, should you decide to come back here.

Secretly, she is a Terraformologist aboard a space station clicking through eons. Small planets lit above pedestals in her laboratory. Inside each one she encodes an image of you. Mountain clavicles. Succulent toes and lakes from your ear hole. Nostril geysers. Each moon, your eye. A seabed smooth as your neck. She leaves you messages in ice, from cracking rock, the gas hisses your name. A spine of desert.

In the morning, before the sheep eat it away, she walks her dog through the fuzz of your cheek. Spread over the South Downs like a love letter.

Biographies

Christopher Hopkins is a Welsh poet living in Faversham, Kent. He has received an IPPY and two Pushcart Prize nominations for his debut chapbook *Take Your Journeys Home*. His second chapbook *The Last Time We Saw Strangers* was released in 2020 and has been nominated for a Pushcart for its poem *Iodine* and the chapbook itself nominated for the CLMP Firecracker Award. He has been widely published including poems in The Morning Star, London Grip, Riggwelter Press, Ghost City Review, The Cortland Review, Indianapolis Review, Mojave River Review, Ink Sweat & Tears and Rust + Moth.

Nick Cirkovic writes fantasy fiction. He lives in London with his wife, his son, and Beethoven.

Claire Scott is an award winning poet who has received multiple Pushcart Prize nominations. Her work has been accepted by the Atlanta Review, Bellevue Literary Review, New Ohio Review, Enizagam and Healing Muse among others. Claire is the author of *Waiting to be Called* and *Until I Couldn't*. She is the co-author of *Unfolding in Light: A Sisters' Journey in Photography and Poetry*.

Annie McCrea holds an Honours and Master's Degree – both in French. She lives in North West Ireland. Her poems have been published in North West Words, Five Muses Press, Channel Literary Magazine and The Honest Ulsterman. She is a member of Derry/Londonderry Writer's Group and a co facilitator of a writing class run by Mental Health.

Bruce Bromley is the author of *Making Figures: Reimagining Body, Sound, and Image in a World That Is Not for U*s. He is a 2013 Pushcart Prize nominee for fiction and teaches writing at New

York University, where he won the Golden Dozen Award for teaching excellence. His poetry, fiction, and essays have appeared in Out Magazine, the Journal of Speculative Philosophy, Gargoyle Magazine, Open Democracy, 3:AM Magazine, and in Environmental Philosophy, among many others.

Dorian Nightingale With a passion for poetry and experimental writing, Dorian has always been fascinated by emotive language and the impact of textures and harmonies within words. Recently he has been particularly influenced by Oulipean constrained writing techniques and has chosen to explore these as well as identifying and evolving new paths and techniques. His inspiration in writing stretches across a broad range of genre from John Cooper Clarke to Philip Glass, from Caravaggio to Progressive Rockers Gazpacho. He is a graduate from New Writing South, Brighton as well as a Masters graduate from the LSE where he studied Politics and Psychology. He lives in East Sussex with his family and when not writing he is clearing up after his teenage children and then recovering by immersing himself in music and cursing the effects of old rugby injuries.

Gret Heffernan is the author of *The Sculptor, The Dark Ansley Trilogy*, and forthcoming lyric essay, *Redneck*. She has just finished writing her first screenplay. She has a degree in English Literature from Vermont College, has attended the BA program at Iowa Writers Workshop, the Faber Academy for poetry and fiction, and is finishing her MA in Creative and Critical Writing at Sussex University. She is the founder of Backlash Press, host of podcasts shows Sketchbook/Notebook and Composed, and co-founder of Edgeland Modern, a pop-up exhibition space and artist collective. Her poetry has been widely published in journals such as Agni and Brittle Star.

Lightning Source UK Ltd.
Milton Keynes UK
UKHW010004210720
366887UK00001B/56